mammalabilia

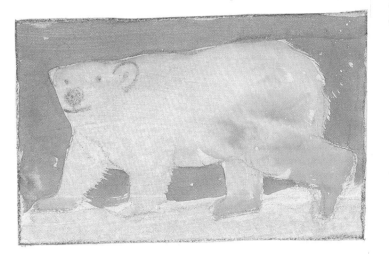

poems and paintings by

Douglas Florian

SCHOLASTIC INC.

New York   Toronto   London   Auckland   Sydney
Mexico City   New Delhi   Hong Kong

Thanks to Sue Nemeroff of Chorley School
for suggesting the phrase "one lump or two"
as regards the camel.

ISBN 0-439-26692-0

12 11 10 9 8 7 6 5 4 3 2 1   1 2 3 4 5 6/0

Printed in the U.S.A.   14

First Scholastic printing, April 2001

The illustrations in this book were done in gouache on primed brown paper bags.
The display type was set in Windsor Bold.
The text type was set in Sabon.
Designed by Kaelin Chappell.

Contents

The Aardvarks

Aardvarks aare odd.
Aardvarks aare staark.
Aardvarks look better
By faar in the daark.

8

The Bactrian Camel

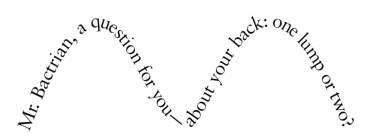

Mr. Bactrian, a question for you— about your back: one lump or two?

The Fox

Clever.
Cunning.
Crafty.
Sly.
A fox composed this poem,
Not I.

The Coyote

I prowl.
I growl.
My howl
Is throaty.
I love
A vowel,
For I am coyo^{oOo}ote.

The Gorilla

A gentle giant
Blessed with grace . . .
It's stilla
Gorilla—
Don't get in its face.

16

The Beaver

Wood-chopper
Tree-dropper
Tail-flopper
Stream-stopper

The Zebras

How many zebras
Do you see?
    I see two zebras.
I see three.
    I see three, too.
I see four.
    I see four, too.
I see more!

19

20

The Lynx

Some people wear fur coats of lynx.
I
think
that
stynx.

The Ibex

The daring ibex risk their necks
On scary, airy mountain treks.
Each one must climb with skill complex,
Or else become an **ex**-ibex.

The Otter

I state most emphatic:
An otter's aquatic.
An otter loves water—
An utter fanatic.
It's most acrobatic,
And quite charismatic.
I state most emphatic:
An otter's aquatic.

The Rhebok

The rhebok's main
Claim to fame
Is its name.

The Elephant

An elephant, rising,
Finds grass appetizing.
And how it loves munchin'
More grass for its luncheon,
As well as its dinner.
It's not getting thinner
And not looking leaner—
It's just growing greener.

The Mule

Voice of the mule: bray
Hue of the mule: bay
Fuel of the mule: hay
Rule of the mule: stay

32

The Tapir

The shape of a tapir
Seems better on paper.

The Lemurs

In Madagascar leaping lemurs breeze through trees without breaking femurs.

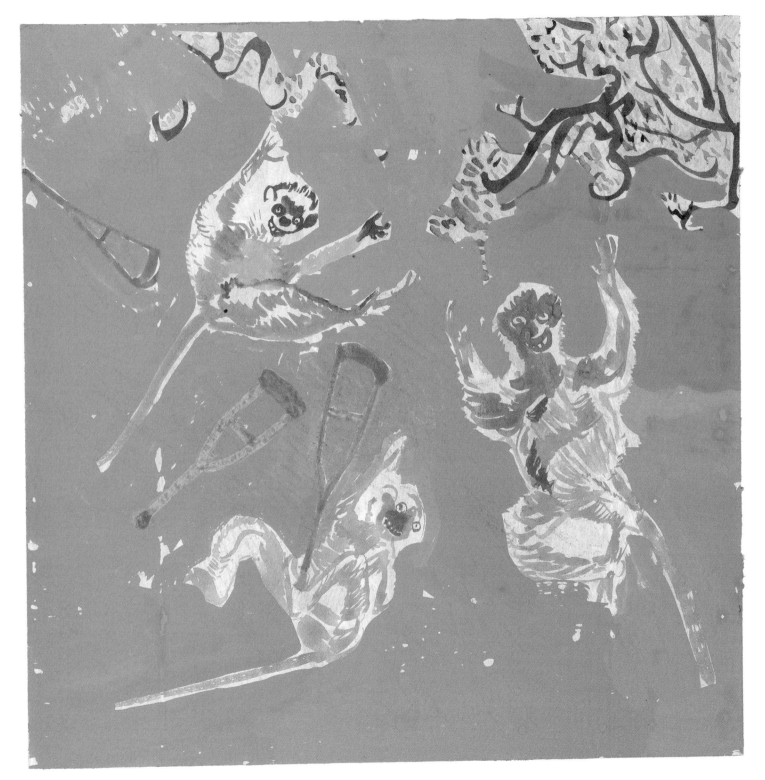

36

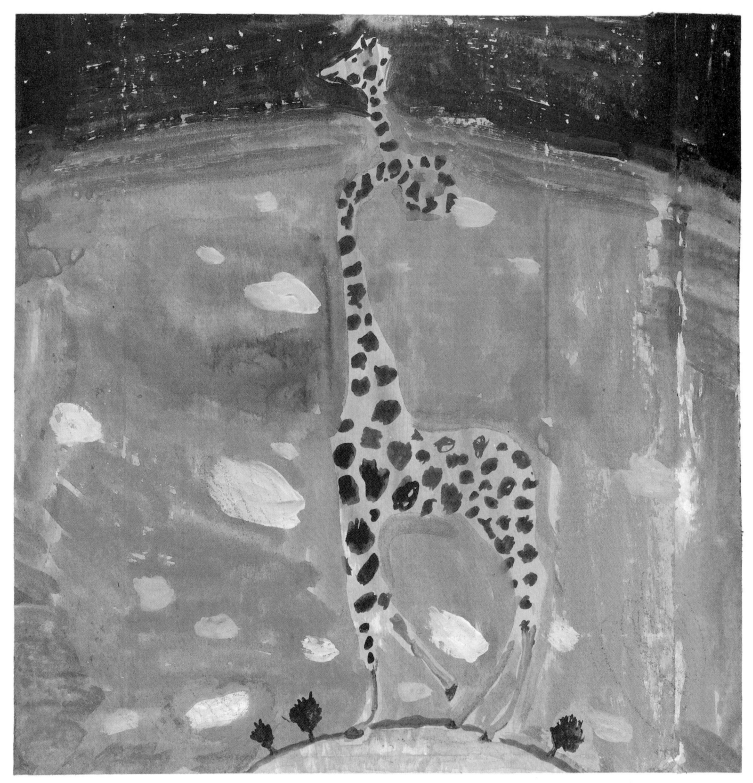

The Giraffe

Rubber-necker
Double-decker
Cloud-checker
Star-trekker

The Hippo

By day the hippo loves to float
On swamps and lakes, much like a boat.
At night from water it retreats,
And eats
      and eats
            and eats
                  and eats.

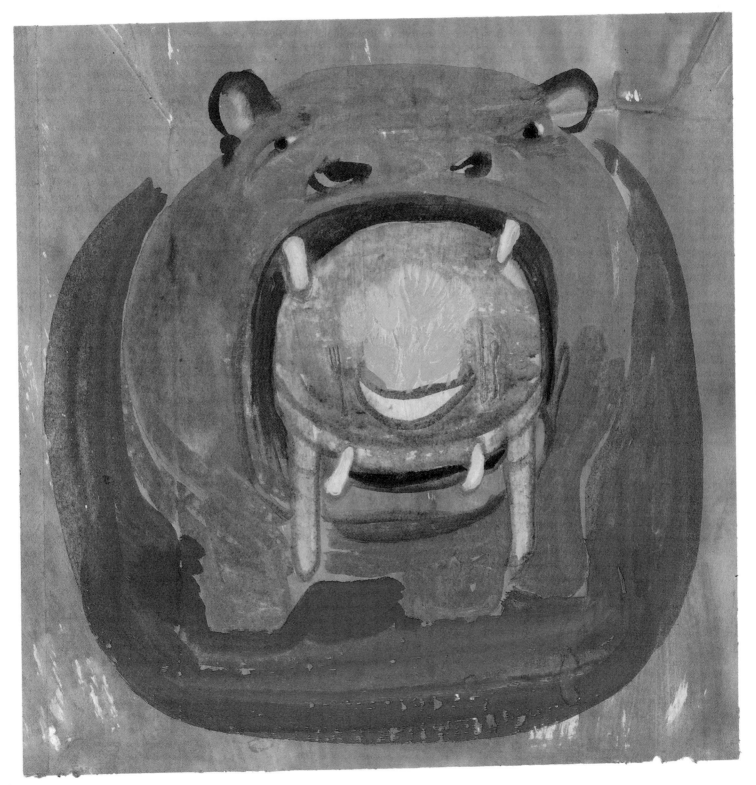

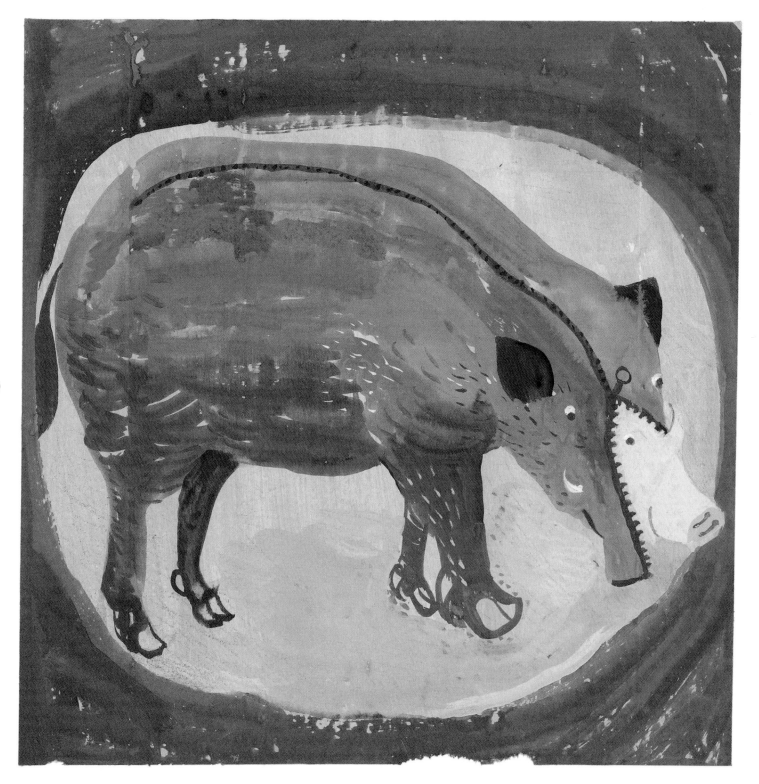

The Boar

The boar at best
Is just a pig

That wears a vest,
And coat, and wig.

The Bear

Come Septem-bear
I sleep, I slum-bear,
Till winter lum-bears
Into spring.
More than that's
Em-bear-rassing.

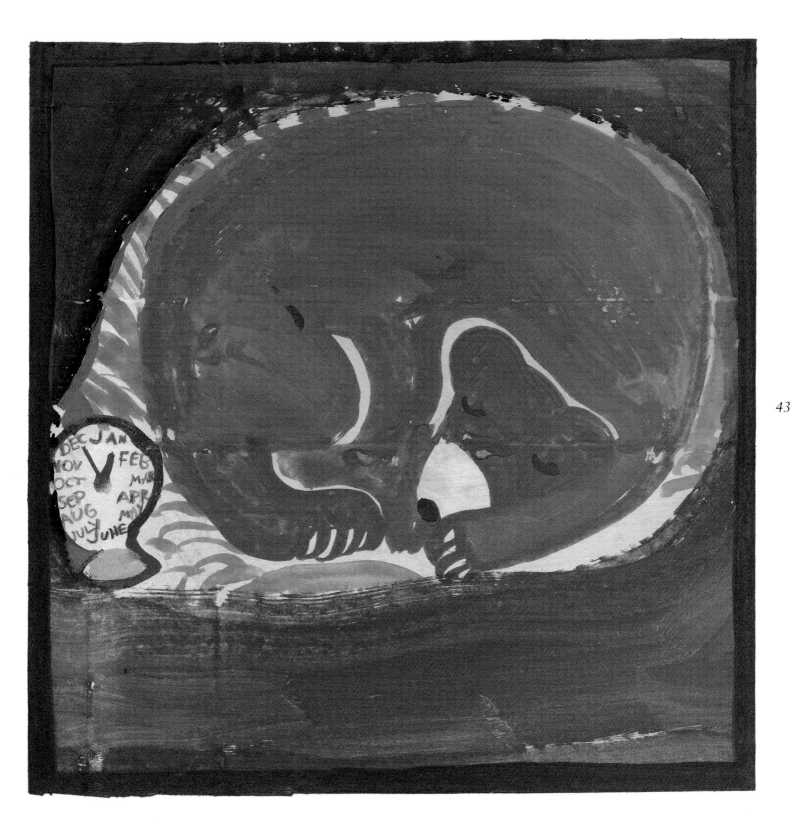

43

The Porcupine

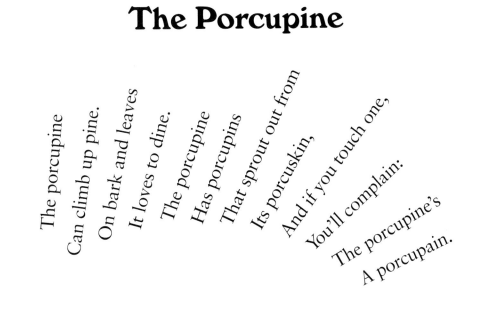

The porcupine
Can climb up pine.
On bark and leaves
It loves to dine.

The porcupine
Has porcupins
That sprout out from
Its porcuskin,

And if you touch one,
You'll complain:
The porcupine's
A porcupain.

The Tiger

I am a cat—come hear me purrrr.
I've many stripes upon my furrrr.
I speed through forests like a blurrrr.
I hunt at night—I am tigerrrr.

47

The illustrations in this book were done in gouache on primed brown paper bags.
The display type was set in Windsor Bold.
The text type was set in Sabon.
Designed by Kaelin Chappell